PEMBURY

Awarded for excellence
to Arts & Libraries

Life in a
GARDEN

Clare Oliver

Evans Brothers Limited

First published in Great Britain in 2002 by Evans Brothers Limited
2A Portman Mansions
Chiltern Street
London W1U 6NR

Copyright © 2002 Steck-Vaughn Company

Project Editors: Sean Dolan, Tamsin Osler, Louise John
Consultant: Michael Chinery
Production Director: Richard Johnson
Illustrated by Stuart Lafford
Designed by Ian Winton

Planned and produced by Discovery Books

British Library Cataloguing in Publication Data
Oliver, Clare
    Life in a garden. - (Microhabitats)
    1. Garden animals - Juvenile literature
    I. Title
    578. 7'554

    ISBN 0 237 523027

Printed in the United States

Contents

The Living Flowerbed

The Flowerbed

Every garden, whether it's your own garden or a public park, is an amazing **microhabitat**. Most of the plants that live there have been planted and cared for by a gardener. They may have been chosen for their colour or delicious smell. You will also find **weeds** and wildlife, such as insects and songbirds, in a garden.

Gardeners can sometimes choose the wildlife in their garden, too. They can grow **species** of flowers that attract butterflies and bees, and plant bushes with berries that attract birds. They can also do things to stop the weeds growing.

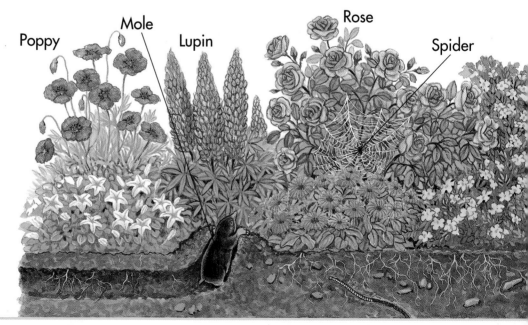

Poppy   Mole   Lupin   Rose   Spider

Sun or Shade

No two gardens are the same. Different soils can affect the plants and wildlife that live there. Things like the weather, traffic and nearby buildings affect the garden, too. Also, if neighbouring plants and trees block out the light, then only plants that like the shade will grow in the garden.

A flowerbed changes all the time. In summer, it is full of life. In winter, the flowers and leaves die and the plants stay dormant until the spring.

Guess What?

The flowers of the nasturtium plant are rich in Vitamin C and iron. They were once used as a remedy against scurvy, a disease caused by lack of Vitamin C.

Gardeners sometimes grow special plants to get rid of garden pests. Roses and sunflowers attract hoverflies and the hoverflies lay their eggs on the flowers. When the eggs hatch, the grubs eat up harmful pests, such as greenflies.

The scents of some flowers have special properties. Lavender is relaxing and is sometimes dried and used to help people sleep.

Red admiral
Buddleia
Thrush
Bee
Worm
Hosta

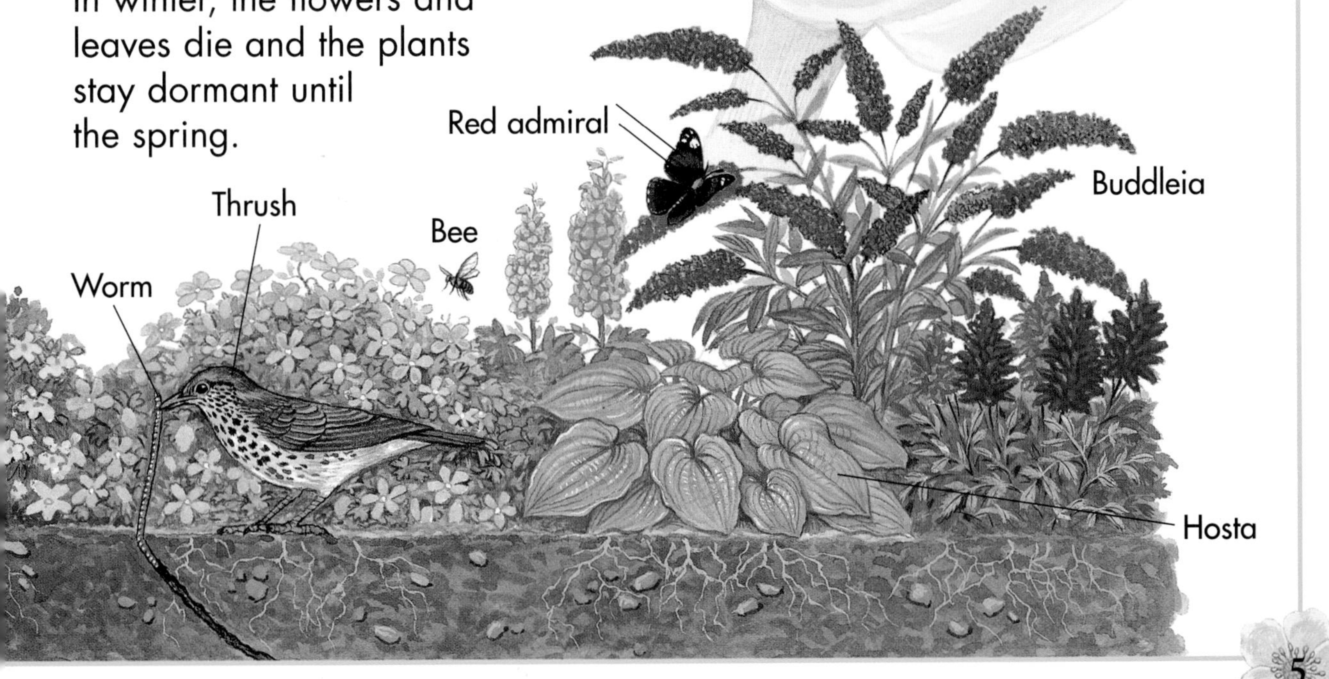

Shapes and Colours

There are thousands of different kinds of flowers. Some grow on single stems like tulips and roses, while others look like spires or umbrellas. Petals can form bowl shapes, pompoms, trumpets or bells.

Standing Tall

Gardeners often plant taller flowers at the back of a flower bed and shorter plants at the front. The tallest ones stand over 1m high and need strong, thick stems to support them. Tall flowers include delphiniums, lupins, and foxgloves. Mid-sized flowers include poppies and geraniums, while tiny crocuses and alpine plants stay close to the ground, out of the wind.

Spring crocuses usually have purple, yellow or white petals.

Plant Life Cycles

Some flowering plants have a life cycle of only one growing season. They produce seeds once and then they die. These plants are called annuals. Plants that live for two growing seasons are called biennials. Perennial plants live for at least three years and often much longer.

Seeds, Bulbs and Tubers

Flowering plants grow from seeds, bulbs or **tubers**. Bulbs and tubers are the part of a plant that is under the ground. They store food for the plant for the next year's growth.

A flowerbed planted with spring flowers: red tulips, white hyacinths, white narcissi and grape (blue) hyacinths.

How Seeds Grow

In spring, warmth from the sun and water trigger the seed to produce roots and shoots. The first roots soon become a tangle that sucks up water and **nutrients** from the soil. Shoots push up through the surface of the soil and leaves unfurl to collect light from the sun.

1. 2. 3. 4.

1. This seed is about to germinate. 2. The outer case of the seed has broken open. 3. A root grows down to anchor the new plant in the soil. 4. A shoot pushes up towards the light and the first leaves begin to grow.

See for Yourself

Grow a miniature garden in a window box. Spell out your name in flowers. Scratch the letters of your name in the soil with a stick. Then put in some seeds and sprinkle over them with more soil. Keep the box moist, but not too wet and wait for the flowers to grow.

8

Pollination

A flower is pollinated when the stigma, or female reproductive organ, of a flower is brushed with powdery **pollen.** The pollen is made by the stamens (male reproductive organs) of a flower and is carried from one flower to another flower of the same type by the wind or by insects. When a flower has been pollinated, the pollen fertilises the egg cells in the ovary and the egg cells then grow into seeds.

Some flowers have female or male parts only. Others, like the lily, have both male and female parts.

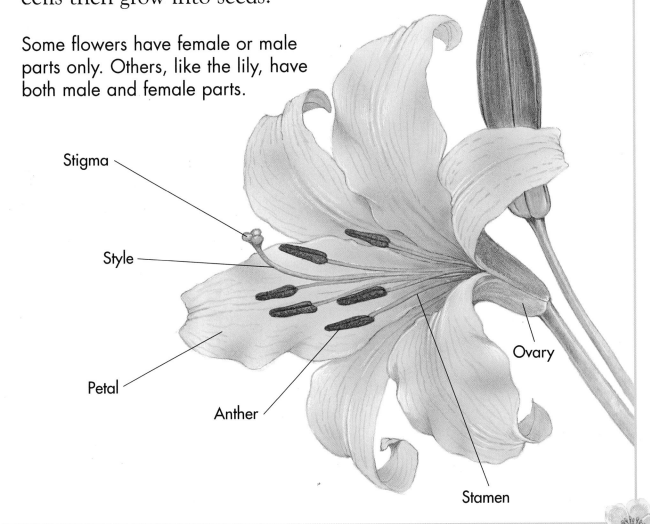

Stigma

Style

Petal

Anther

Ovary

Stamen

Life in the Soil

Kinds of Soil

The soil in the garden provides the moisture and nutrients the plants need. Soil can be chalky, sandy, crumbly or like clay. Different plants prefer different kinds of soil.

Millipedes like moist soil and mainly feed on rotting plants. Gardeners think they are pests because they can damage seedlings and soft shoots.

Gardeners can improve, or **fertilise**, the soil by mixing in compost, a soil-like material of rotted vegetable and plant matter. They can also cover it with a mulch, such as a layer of bark chippings or cocoa pods. Mulching helps keep in moisture and helps stop the growth of weeds.

Natural Helpers

Earthworms, woodlice, millipedes and tiny mites feed on decaying leaves and animal matter in the soil. These creatures break up the soil as they tunnel through it, which allows plant roots to spread easily and rainwater to drain away. It also allows nutrients to spread through the soil.

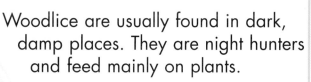

Woodlice are usually found in dark, damp places. They are night hunters and feed mainly on plants.

Guess What?

Woodlice, also known as sow bugs, are not insects. They belong to a group of animals called crustaceans and are more closely related to crabs than beetles!

A type of Australian earthworm can grow to 3.3m in length!

Worms can survive being cut in two, but it is not true that they do not feel pain.

Fungi and bacteria help matter decompose, or rot, in the soil. The waste of the creatures that live in the soil acts as a natural compost, too.

Food Farms

Ants often make their nests in soil. They feed on honeydew, a sticky, sugary substance produced by **aphids**, which are tiny insects not much bigger than a pin head. The ants 'farm' the aphids like cattle, fighting off their **predators** for them and 'milking' them for their honeydew. Aphids can do serious damage to plants by sucking out the sap but ants can actually help plants by adding air to the soil when they tunnel.

These red ants are looking after bean aphids. Ants encourage aphids to give out honeydew by 'tickling' them with their antennae.

Slimy Trails

Slugs and snails crawl about on a large, muscular foot. Their soft bodies are almost identical, except that snails carry a shell on their back. They belong to a group of **molluscs** called **gastropods**.

Both slugs and snails can damage gardens. Their favourite foods include lilies and tulips, but just about any soft, fleshy plant matter will do.

Slugs and snails harm leaves by scraping them with their rough tongues and by leaving a sticky slime behind.

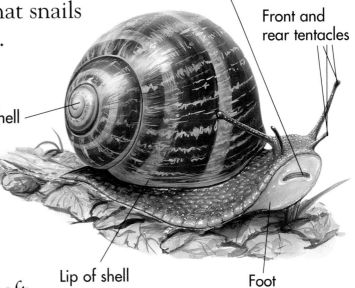

Mouth and rasping tongue

Front and rear tentacles

Shell

Lip of shell

Foot

Guess What?

An ant's nest may contain more than 100,000 ants.

Ants may bite in self-defence. Some types even squirt out acid.

Snails and slugs are both gastropods. This word actually means 'belly foot'!

Slugs and snails can lay as many as 200 eggs at a time.

Crawling Hunters

Night and day, thousands of creatures hunt in the flowerbed. The main predators are beetles, earwigs and centipedes. Ladybirds are the most commonly seen flowerbed **beetles**, with their shiny red, orange or yellow shell with black polka dots.

Ladybirds are the gardener's friend, and so are their larvae (the young that hatch from the ladybirds' eggs). Both eat aphids and other soft-bodied pests that feast on flowers and stems. Earwigs eat aphids, but they also nibble garden plants, so they are not quite so welcome.

The antennae of the male longhorn beetle is sometimes longer than its body. Many species are found on garden flowers.

Underground

Beneath the soil, soldier beetle larvae and centipedes wriggle about in search of **prey** to feed on. Centipedes, which have amazingly powerful jaws, prefer to hunt at night. Centipedes are not insects because they don't have six legs. They don't have exactly 100 legs either, despite their name.

Earwigs are very protective mothers. They lick their eggs clean and guard them from predators.

Life on a Plant

Bugs

You may call all little creepy-crawly creatures **'bugs'** but, in fact, bugs are a special group of insects that have a beak for sucking up liquids such as plant juices – or blood! Sap-sucking bugs include whiteflies and common aphids (commonly known as greenflies). Gardeners think they are pests because they suck up the juices of leaves, stems and flowers. Sap-sucking insects can spread plant diseases from one flower to another. The diseases can permanently damage the leaves and cause poor growth.

Sap-sucking bugs have narrow tubes to suck up plant and animal juices.

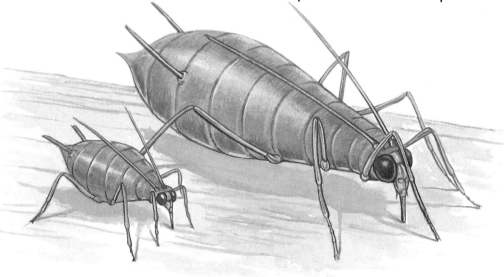

Jumping Bugs

Most bugs have wings, but some are also excellent jumpers, such as froghoppers and leafhoppers. You might not see their very quick jumps but you are sure to spot the froghopper's larvae, or at least the frothy 'cuckoo spit' where they hide and keep their soft bodies safe and moist.

Guess What?

An aphid can produce 50 babies in a week. Within seven days they will all have grown to adulthood and be ready to breed themselves.

Shield bugs are often known as stink bugs because they ward off predators by making a disgusting smell!

The bug family includes the world's loudest insects, cicadas, which make their distinctive 'song' by vibrating membranes on their abdomen.

Shield bugs get their name from the shape of their bodies.

Web Weavers

On a dewy morning, you can often see glistening webs that have been spun between plants in the garden. These are spun by orb weaver spiders as a sticky net to trap flies and other prey in mid-air. The web is not sticky enough to hold the prey for long, so the spider lies in wait, ready to attack. It paralyses its prey with a poisonous bite and wraps it in silken threads.

The most common webs are round orb webs. They have to be freshly spun each day, or at least repaired.

Making a web

1. The spider spins a bridge between two points.

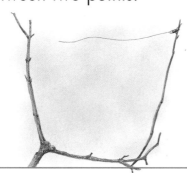

2. The spider drops down to attach one of the bridge threads to a point below.

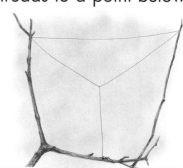

Spider Features

Spiders are not insects, because they have eight legs. They belong to a group of animals called **arachnids**. All spiders are hunters, but not all spiders spin webs to catch prey. Wolf spiders outrun their prey, while jumping spiders leap at theirs.

Guess What?

When silk first comes out of the spider, it is still runny. It sets hard in the air.

The male ladybird spider is less than a quarter of the size of his mate!

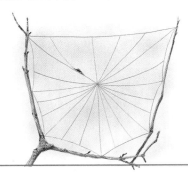

Crab spiders can camouflage themselves by gradually changing their colour to that of the flower petals where they hide. It normally takes them 4 or 5 days to change from one colour to another.

3. It adds threads around the edge of the web and then moves into the centre.

4. It makes a spiral of sticky threads. Each web can have up to 30m of silk in it.

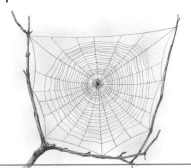

On the Wing

Stripes for Danger

In summer, a garden contains lots of food for bees. Most flowers are pollinated by honeybees or their larger relatives, the bumblebees. Like ants, honeybees live together in colonies. The female workers fetch pollen and nectar, the sugary liquid inside a flower, for their larvae and 'dance' by making a pattern of movements to tell other bees where food is! The nectar is turned into sweet, syrupy honey.

A honeybee collects pollen from a flower.

Spot the Difference

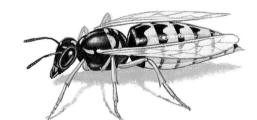

The honeybee is not very furry for a bee. Its stripes are duller than a wasp's.

Wasps are longer and more slender than honeybees. Their shiny bodies are not as furry.

Wasps

Both bees and wasps can give a nasty sting in self-defence. Like bees, many wasps are striped. Like bees, adult wasps feed on sugary nectar. In other ways, though, bees and wasps are quite different. Wasps feed their babies on caterpillars and other insects and have less hairy bodies. The large hornet wasp is very common in Great Britain.

The wasps inside this nest are looking after the larvae and eggs inside their cells.

Stand very still if you are watching bees or wasps and don't get too close. They can give you a very painful sting.

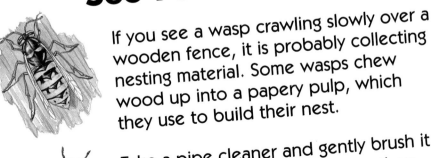

See For Yourself

If you see a wasp crawling slowly over a wooden fence, it is probably collecting nesting material. Some wasps chew wood up into a papery pulp, which they use to build their nest.

Take a pipe cleaner and gently brush it against the stamens of a flower, then check it for pollen. See how a furry bee's legs pick up pollen?

Fluttering Flies

Many garden flies wear a sneaky disguise. The hoverfly's black and yellow colouring makes it look just like a wasp, and so birds and other predators keep away, to avoid getting stung. Thick-headed flies use the same trick, though some look more like bees than wasps. These flies are very busy during the day, when flowers are fully open.

Flowers attract pollinating insects like this hoverfly with their bright petals, special markings or strong scents.

Losing Legs

At twilight, lacewings and craneflies come out to feed. Normally, long, gangly craneflies have six legs, but they often lose one or two in a spider's web! Craneflies do not live very long as adults, but they can survive for years underground as larvae or leatherjackets. Leatherjackets are garden pests, eating the roots of precious plants.

There are about 15 thousand different types of cranefly.

It is no wonder common lacewings have bright green bodies: they feed on plump, green aphids. They get their name because of their see-through, lacy wings.

Guess What?

Craneflies are sometimes called 'Daddy-long-legs'. They date back as far as prehistoric times.

Thick-headed fly larvae are not very polite. They lay their eggs on the body of a bee or a wasp. When they hatch, the grubs burrow into the host's body and eat it from the inside out!

Honey guides are markings on flowers. They look like runway lights at the airport. They guide insects to the nectar.

23

Beautiful Butterflies

Caterpillars are the larvae of butterflies or moths. Once they have made this change (a process called metamorphosis), they benefit flowering plants and sip nectar from the plants.

Caterpillars munch their way thr leaves and stems, causing a lot damage to the garden.

Butterflies and moths have special, long, tube-like mouths to make this easy for them. They also pick up pollen on their bodies and as they move on to other flowers, these are pollinated and seeds can begin to grow.

Caterpillars turn themselves into chrysalises before they become butterflies.

Great Attractors

Gardeners often plant very scented flowers to attract butterflies. Flowers of this kind include lavender, sweet william and, of course, the butterfly bush (buddleia).

Guess What?

Butterflies and moths shimmer when light reflects from the tiny scales that cover their wings.

Butterflies differ from other flies in that they have two pairs of wings, not one.

Most moth caterpillars spend the chrysalis stage (the resting state between caterpillar and moth) inside a silken cocoon.

There are about 500 species of swallowtail worldwide. Most species have little 'tails' on their rear wings.

Butterflies come in an amazing range of colours – white, blue, yellow, black, and red. Some are like moths, with brown colouring to act as a **camouflage** against predators.

Garden Birds

All sorts of birds visit the garden, especially in spring and summer. Thrushes, starlings, and blackbirds dig for juicy worms. The birds have a good sense of hearing and they know just where to strike. They eat fruit and berries, too. Other insect-eating birds include swallows, warblers, and woodpeckers. They are good for the garden because they eat aphids, caterpillars and other plant-eating pests.

Pigeons (above) feed on seeds and leaves, whereas thrushes (below) feed on worms, snails, insects and fruit.

Feeding the Birds

In autumn, small garden birds such as finches and titmice often come to the garden to feed on plants with seeds or fruits, such as rose hips. You can attract the birds by putting up a hanging bird feeder filled with seeds, nuts, and different grains.

(Right) Finches, nuthatches and tits are attracted to hanging bird feeders.

See For Yourself

Natural bird food is scarce in winter. Put out piles of different seeds and see which bird eats what. Leave a dish of water, too, for the birds to drink and bathe in. But be careful to place them out of reach of cats!

Put lots of seeds, nuts, and raisins in a bowl. Ask an adult to pour melted lard or fat over it and then mix it all together. When the bird cake is cool, cut slices for the birds. Why not add pieces of apple or bacon strips to the mix?

Borrow a birdsong tape from your local library and learn to identify garden visitors by ear alone.

Other Visitors

Furry Creatures

When small **mammals** visit the garden, they can cause a lot of damage. Moles tunnel underground for juicy worms. They are expert diggers, with shovel-shaped front paws that are perfect for the job. Squirrels dig, too, especially for tender bulbs. In late summer, you might spot a shy wood or harvest mouse in a flowerbed, attracted by all the seeds and berries.

Moles can leave messy piles of soil around, damage plants, and greatly reduce the worm population in a garden.

Lying in Wait

A visiting fox might sleep among the foliage of the plants in a garden. The sheltered bed also hides cats waiting to pounce on birds or mice, too. Some gardeners use sprays or scarecrows to try to keep animal pests away from their flowerbeds.

The harvest mouse is an expert climber. It feeds on seeds, grasses, and parts of flowers.

See For Yourself

Winter is the best time to look for signs of animal visitors. Look for these footprints in the snow:

Hedgehog

Squirrel

Rabbit

Fox

Glossary

Aphids: Small, soft-bodied insects, such as greenfly. Aphids are bugs. They have a beak-like mouth for piercing plant stems and sucking up plant sap (juice).

Arachnids: Animals that have eight legs and two parts to their body. Spiders and scorpions are types of arachnid.

Beetles: Insects with strong jaws for biting. An adult beetle's wings are usually protected by hard, shiny wing cases.

Bugs: Insects that only feed on liquids, using a beak-like mouth to pierce and suck. An adult bug's front wings cross over on its back to make an 'X' shape.

Camouflage: Colouring, or a means of disguise, that makes an animal blend in with its surroundings so that it is more difficult for predators to see.

Fertilise: To make something able to produce fruit, seeds, or offspring.

Gastropods: Molluscs that have a large, muscular foot for moving along on. Snails and slugs are both gastropods.

Larva: An insect baby, such as a beetle grub or a caterpillar, that looks nothing like its parent.

Mammals: Warm-blooded animals, such as foxes or mice, that give birth to live young and feed them on mother's milk.

Microhabitat: A small, specialised place, such as a garden or a freshwater pond, where particular animals live and plants grow.

Molluscs: Boneless animals with soft bodies that need to be kept damp and are sometimes protected by a shell. Snails, mussels, and octopuses are all types of molluscs.

Nutrients: The minerals and other substances in soil that nourish or feed a plant and help it to grow.

Pollen: A powder produced by the male parts of a flower. Pollen is usually yellow. For a plant to be fertilised and able to produce a seed, pollen has to be brushed on to its female parts.

Predators: Animals that hunt other animals for food.

Prey: Animals that are hunted by other animals for food.

Species: A type of animal or plant; for example the wood ant is a species of ant.

Tubers: Swollen underground roots or stems. Tubers can produce tiny buds that will eventually grow into new plants. Plants that grow from tubers include dahlias, irises and potatoes.

Weeds: Plants that spring up in gardens and grow where they are not wanted. Gardeners try to get rid of weeds because they use up nutrients and water in the soil. They can also strangle other plants or block out their light.

Acknowledgements

The publishers would like to thank the following for permission to reproduce their pictures:
Cover: Bruce Coleman Collection; p.6t: Geoff Kidd/Oxford Scientific Films; p.6b: Robert P. Carr/Bruce Coleman; p.10: Dan Griggs/NHPA; p.11: N.A. Callow/NHPA; p.12: K.G. Prestom-Mafham/Premaphotos Wildlife; p.13: Chris Fairclough Picture Library; p.14: J. Brackenbury/Bruce Coleman; p.15: Tim Shepherd/Oxford Scientific Films; p.16: G.J. Cambridge/NHPA; p.18: Michael Leach/Oxford Scientific Films; p.20: Stephen Dalton/NHPA; p.21: Kim Taylor/Bruce Coleman; p.22: N.A. Callow/NHPA; p.23t: Martin Garwood/NHPA; p.23b: J. Brackenbury/Bruce Coleman; p.24t: John Shaw/NHPA; p.24b: Jane Burton/Bruce Coleman; p.25: Photodisc; p.26t: Alberto Nardi/NHPA; p.26b: Kim Taylor/Bruce Coleman; p.27: Chris Fairclough/Discovery Picture Library; p.28: Hans Reinhard/Bruce Coleman; p.29: Joe Blossom/NHPA.

Index